DIFFERENT KINDS OF PRAYERS

EVANGELIST INNOCENT

Unless otherwise noted, scriptures quoted are from the New King James Version of the Bible. Copyright © 1979, 1980, 1982, 1985 by Thomas Nelson Inc. Used by permission. All rights reserved.

Copyright © 2007 by Evangelist Innocent
All rights reserved.

Different Kinds Of Prayers
ISBN: 978-1-921698-12-5 (print)
ISBN: 978-1-921698-47-7 (ebook)

No part of this publication may be reproduced, stored in a retrieval system, or transmitted in any form or by any means-electronic, mechanical, photocopying, recording, or otherwise-without the prior written permission of the publisher and copyrighters.

FORWARD

In this series, the writer, Evangelist Innocent Mokwe wants us to know that the destiny of the church is being decided now on our knees. In the calendar and agenda of God, every year is unique, significant and eventful. No year is either a coincidence or an emergency, but a well planned, packaged and coordinated handwork of God to fulfil special things in the lives of individuals, institutions and nations according to His eternal purposes. The present army that God is raising there shall be no children; there shall be no small men. All big men shall be warriors. All small men shall be warriors. No matter your size or position, you shall be called a warrior.

This is the reason the present Church has to go through a second touch or Gilgal experiences. In spite of all the jumping and shouting, many still go back and feel empty because every Christian is constantly facing some spiritual warfare. The world, flesh and devil always wage war to discourage the believer in his faith and if possible, silence or claim his soul. Often some very dear children of God are fatally wounded in such warfare due to their failure to understand and apply spiritual truth.

In the present army, God is raising them on their knees; there is no automatic qualification, just as you chose only 300 men for the Gideon army out of 32,000 that responded to the call. It is not everyone in church that will be recruited. Your every action, in the practical, is either qualifying or disqualifying you from the army. We are talking about the invasion of serious minded people who know their God and are ready to do exploits. The bible says that a king or master, no matter how great he is, is not better than a servant if he is still a child. Dear reader, there are scriptural truths you may have overlooked to your own peril. When you know spiritual truth, you will receive them. You can only possess in prayer as far as your eyes (of faith) can see.

This book in your hand will help you to understand your spiritual authority as a believer and the overcoming power that God Almighty has given you to use and crush the enemy and "legally" to recover all. May the Holy Spirit inspired messages in these books change your situation until God's full purpose for your life is actualized.

Rev Emmau. Ubani, General Overseer
Jesus Messengers Ministries Inc (Home Of Missions)
NO 1 JESUS MESSENGERS BY -PASS
OFF 2ND ARMY GATE ONITSHA -
ENUGU EXPRESSWAY
ONITSHA ANAMBRA STATE NIGERIA
+234-8034077902

ACKNOWLEDGEMENT

I want to thank God Almighty for giving me the privilege, the unction and the power to write this book. I give Him all the praise and adoration.

May His name be highly lifted up, in the name of Jesus Christ. I also thank Him for the other books that I have written, and more to be written. I believe every man and woman reading this book will not be a double-minded person want to assure you, this book was not written by my own power but by the power of the Holy Spirit. I hope after reading this book, may your life be transformed.

May God bless you and keep you always, in Jesus mighty name.

CONTENTS

FORWARD -- 3

ACKNOWLEDGEMENT -- 6

CONTENTS --- 7

INTRODUCTION -- 1

PART 1   DIFFERENT KINDS OF PRAYERS ---------- 7
   Prayer For Forgiveness And Confession --------------- 9
   Prayer For Healing --- 13
   Prayer For Divine Connection --------------------------- 15
   Prayer For Open Doors ----------------------------------- 17
   Prayer For Breakthrough --------------------------------- 19

PART 2   DIFFERENT KINDS OF PRAYERS -------- 23
   Prayer Against The Devourer ---------------------------- 23
   Prayer To Overcome The Habit Of Making Rash
   Promises To God --- 24
   Prayer For Paying Your Tithes -------------------------- 26
   Prayer For Helping The Poor ---------------------------- 29
   Prayer For Your Marriage Life --------------------------- 32
   Prayer For Married Couples ----------------------------- 33
   Prayer For The Fruit Of The Womb -------------------- 35
   Prayer For Thanksgiving --------------------------------- 37
   Prayer To Know Your Vision ----------------------------- 40
   Prayer To Know Your Ministry --------------------------- 42
   Prayer To Turn Your Weaknesses To Strength --- 44

Prayer To Read And To Understand The Word Of God --46
Prayer To Speak In Tongues ----------------------------48
Prayer To Love One Another ----------------------------50
Prayer Against Discrimination --------------------------51
Prayer To See The Face Of God ------------------------53
Prayer To Perform Miracles -----------------------------54
Prayer To Increase Your Faith In God ----------------56
Prayer For Grace --58

PART 3 DIFFERENT KINDS OF PRAYERS --------61
Prayer For Churches -------------------------------------61
Prayer For Nations ---------------------------------------64
Prayer For Giving To God -------------------------------66
Prayer For Travelling ------------------------------------68
Prayer To Pay All Your Debts --------------------------69
Prayer For Making Use Of Your Gifts -----------------71
Prayer For Your Friends --------------------------------73
Prayer To Understand And To Know When God Speaks --75
Prayer For An Increase ---------------------------------76
Prayer For Families --------------------------------------77
Prayer To Have The Mind Of Christ -------------------79
Prayer For Favour --80
Prayer For Understanding In Our Studies -----------81
Prayer To Put Your Trust In God -----------------------82
Prayer To Be Complete In God ------------------------83
Prayer For Destiny ---------------------------------------84

PART 4 DIFFERENT KINDS OF PRAYERS --------85
Prayer To Break Every Chain Of Bondage ----------85
Prayer For Breaking Every Yoke ----------------------86

Prayer For Breaking Every Barrenness -------------- 87
Prayer For Churches To Be In Unity ----------------- 88
Prayer For Nations To Be In Unity ------------------- 90
Prayer For Restoration --------------------------------- 92
Prayer To Set The Captives Free -------------------- 94
Prayer Against Every Hindrance ---------------------- 95

PART 5   THE BENEFITS OF PRAYER --------------- 97

EPILOGUE --- 101

WORD OF ENCOURAGEMENT ------------------------ 103

ABOUT THE AUTHOR ---------------------------------- 109

LIST OF OTHER BOOKS WRITTEN BY THE AUTHOR -- 113

INTRODUCTION

What is prayer? It is a communication between Man and God. It is the living proof of God's miraculous wonders in our lives. When we obey God's word and seek His face through prayer, God will confirm His word in season and out of season. Prayer is supernatural and it is strength in our lives. Prayer is the key that moves mountains. When we want to pray we must pray with all our heart. We do not pray like a hypocrite. Rather we must pray according to God's principles.

Jesus tells us in Matthew 6:5-13, "And when you pray, you shall not be like the hypocrites. For they love to pray standing in the synagogues and on the corners of the streets, that they may be seen by men. Assuredly, I say to you, they have their reward.

But you, when you pray, go into your room, and when you have shut your door, pray to your Father who is in the secret place; and your Father who sees in secret will reward you openly. And when you pray, do not use vain repetitions as the heathen do. For they think that they will be heard for their many words. "Therefore do not be like them. For your Father knows the things you have need of before you ask Him. In this manner, therefore, pray :

>Our Father in heaven,
>Hallowed be Your name
>Your kingdom come
>Your will be done
>On earth as it is in heaven.
>Give us this day our daily bread
>And forgive us our debts,
>As we forgive our debtors.
>And do not lead us into temptation,
>But deliver us from the evil one.
>For Yours is the kingdom and

the power and the glory forever. Amen.""

The Hour Of Prayer

Your word O LORD said, it shall come to pass, if you diligently obey the voice of the LORD your God, to observe carefully all His commandments which I command you today, that the LORD your God will set you high above all nations of the earth. And all these blessings shall come upon you and overtake you because you obey the voice of the LORD your God:

"Blessed shall you be in the city, and blessed shall you be in the country. Blessed shall be the fruit of your body, the produce of your ground and the increase of your herds, the increase of your cattle and the offspring of your flocks. Blessed shall be your basket and your kneading bowl. Blessed shall you be when you come in, and blessed shall you be when you go out. The LORD will cause your enemies who rise against you to be defeated before your face; they shall come out against you one way and flee before you seven ways.

The LORD will command the blessing on you in your storehouses and in all to which you set your hand, and He will bless you in the land which the LORD your God is giving you. The LORD will establish you as a holy people to Himself, just as He has sworn to you, if you keep the commandments of the LORD your God and walk in His ways.

Then all peoples of the earth shall see that you are called by the name of the LORD, and they shall be afraid of you. And the LORD will grant you plenty of goods, in the fruit of your body, in the increase of your livestock, and in the produce of your ground, in the land of which the LORD swore to your fathers to give you. The LORD will open to you His good treasure, the heavens, to give the rain to your land in its season, and to bless all the work of your hand. You shall lend to many nations, but you shall not borrow. And the LORD will make you the head and not the tail; you shall be above only, and not be beneath, if you heed the commandments of the LORD your God, which I command you today, and are careful to observe them. So you shall not turn aside from any of the words which I command you this day, to the right or the left, to go after other gods to serve them."

O LORD, give us the grace to diligently obey Your voice and to observe carefully all the commandments which You have commanded us today, in Jesus mighty name we pray. Amen.

PART 1

Different Kinds Of Prayers

In general, prayer has been taken to be a form of religious practice that seeks to activate a volitional connection to some greater power in the universe through deliberate practice. Prayer may be either individual or communal and take place in public or in private. It may involve the use of words or song. When language is used, prayer may take the form of a hymn or a spontaneous utterance in the praying person. There are different forms of prayer such as petitionary prayer, prayers of supplication, thanksgiving, and worship or praise.

Prayer may be directed towards a spirit, deceased person or lofty idea for the purpose of worshipping, requesting guidance, requesting assistance, confessing sins or to express one's thoughts and emotions. Thus, people pray for many reasons such as for personal benefit or for the sake of others.

Prayer is communication between Man and God. It is the living proof of God's miraculous wonders in our lives. When we obey God's word and seek His face through prayer, God will confirm His word in season and out of season. Prayer is a supernatural strength in our lives. It is God's miraculous wonders which give birth to hope in our lives. It is the living proof that will cause God to hear our voice and answer our prayer. When we close our mouth and not be prayerful God will not answer us. Beloved, there is time to lift up our voice and pray to God. I know there is time for meditation but there is also time to lift up our voice to God.

Psalm 150 says, "Praise the LORD! Praise God in His sanctuary; Praise Him in His mighty firmament! Praise Him for His mighty acts; Praise

Him according to His excellent greatness! Praise Him with the sound of the trumpet; Praise Him with the lute and harp! Praise Him with the timbrel and dance; Praise Him with stringed instruments and flutes! Praise Him with loud cymbals; Praise Him with clashing cymbals! Let everything that has breath praise the LORD. Praise the LORD!"

Prayer For Forgiveness And Confession

And be kind to one another, tender hearted, forgiving one another, even as God in Christ forgave you.

(Ephesians 4:32)

Bearing with one another, and forgiving one another, if anyone has a complaint against another; even as Christ forgave you, so you also must do.

(Colossians 3:13

If we say that we have no sin, we deceive ourselves, and the truth is not in us. If we confess our sins, He is faithful and just to forgive us our sins and to cleanse us from all unrighteousness. If we say that we have not sinned, we make Him a liar, and His word is not in us.

(1 John 1:8-10)

If My people who are called by My name will humble themselves, and pray and seek My face, and turn from their wicked ways, then I will hear from heaven, and will forgive their sin and heal their land.

(1 Chronicles 7:14)

Blessed is he whose transgression is forgiven, whose sin is covered.

(Psalm 32:1)

And forgive us our debts, As we forgive our debtors.

(Matthew 6:12)

O LORD, forgive us from all our iniquities done knowingly or unknowingly. Your word says that for all have sinned and come short of the glory of God. The wages of sin is death but the gift of God is eternal life through Jesus Christ our Lord and Saviour. Righteousness exalts a nation, but sin is a reproach to any people. Your word says in Isaiah 1:18, ""Come now, and let us reason together," Says the LORD, "Though your sins are like scarlet, they shall be as white as snow; though they are red like crimson, they shall be as wool."

We ask Thee O LORD to give us the grace to forgive those who have hurt us and done us wrong because Your word says that we are to be kind to one another, tender hearted, forgiving one another, even as God in Christ forgave us. O LORD, I forgive every person who has sinned against me in Jesus mighty name. Amen

Now Pray This Prayer

Jesus said, "Therefore do not be like them. For your Father knows the things you have need of before you ask Him. In this manner, therefore, pray: Our Father in heaven, hallowed be Your name. Your kingdom come. Your will be done on earth as it is in heaven. Give us this day our daily bread. And forgive us our debts, as we forgive our debtors. And do not lead us into temptation, but deliver us from the evil one. For Yours is the kingdom and the power and the glory forever. Amen. "For if you forgive men their trespasses, your heavenly Father will also forgive you. But if you do not forgive men their trespasses, neither will your heavenly Father forgive your trespasses."

We ask all these through Jesus Christ our personal Lord and Saviour. Amen.

Prayer For Healing

Isaiah 53:5-6 says, "But He was wounded for our transgressions, He was bruised for our iniquities; the chastisement for our peace was upon Him, and by His stripes we are healed. All we like sheep have gone astray; We have turned, every one, to his own way; And the LORD has laid on Him the iniquity of us all."

Your word says in 1 Peter 2:24-25, "who Himself bore our sins in His own body on the tree, that we, having died to sins, might live for righteousness—by whose stripes you were healed. For you were like sheep going astray, but have now returned to the Shepherd and Overseer of your souls."

The book of Isaiah said in those days that Hezekiah was sick and near death. And Isaiah the prophet, the son of Amoz, went to him and said to him, "Thus says the LORD: 'Set your house in order, for you shall die and not live.'" Then Hezekiah turned his face toward the wall, and prayed to the

LORD, and said, "Remember now, O LORD, I pray, how I have walked before You in truth and with a loyal heart, and have done what is good in Your sight." And Hezekiah wept bitterly. And the word of the LORD came to Isaiah, saying, "Go and tell Hezekiah, 'Thus says the LORD, the God of David your father: "I have heard your prayer, I have seen your tears; surely I will add to your days fifteen years. I will deliver you and this city from the hand of the king of Assyria, and I will defend this city."' And this is the sign to you from the LORD, that the LORD will do this thing which He has spoken: Behold, I will bring the shadow on the sundial, which has gone down with the sun on the sundial of Ahaz, ten degrees backward." So the sun returned ten degrees on the dial by which it had gone down."

Now Pray This Prayer

O LORD, heal me in every area of my life. Heal me in my marriage life. Heal me in my business. Heal me in my ministry. Heal me in my wealth. Heal me in my health. Heal me in my financial breakthrough. Heal me in my faith in You. Heal me in my commitment to You. Heal me in my capacity in You. Heal me in my influence in God. Heal me to understand your word. Heal me to speak like an oracle of God. Heal me to speak the possibilities in God and not in the impossibilities. Heal me so that I can continue to put all my trust in You. Heal me so that I can forgive all my enemies. Heal me so that I will be filled with the inspiration of the Holy Ghost. Heal me so that I will not be afraid of my enemies. Heal me so that I will not be a victim of the enemies, rather be a victor of them in Jesus mighty name. Amen.

Prayer For Divine Connection

Acts 9:27-30 says, "But Barnabas took him and brought him to the apostles. And he declared to them how he had seen the Lord on the road, and that He had spoken to him, and how he had preached boldly at Damascus in the name of Jesus. So he was with them at Jerusalem, coming in and going out. And he spoke boldly in the name of the Lord Jesus and disputed against the Hellenists, but they attempted to kill him. When the brethren found out, they brought him down to Caesarea and sent him out to Tarsus."

> *The steps of a good man are ordered by the LORD, and He delights in his way. Though he fall, he shall not be utterly cast down; For the LORD upholds him with His hand.*
>
> *(Psalm 37:23-24)*

Divine connection is the confirmation of God's word to come to pass in our lives. It is God's miracle wonder which will place us at the right place, at the right time. When we obey God's word, He will confirm His word in us.

Beloved, God's eyes are on you because He sees all the sons of men from the place of His dwelling. His hands are not shortened that He cannot save you nor His ear heavy that He cannot hear you.

The Hour Of Prayer

O LORD, I need Your divine connection in my life. I need men and women who will help me to fulfil my destiny in life. I need men and women who will compete to do me good, wherever I may be.

I need your divine connection to show up in my business, in my marriage life, in the ministry and in my financial breakthrough, in Jesus name. Amen.

Prayer For Open Doors

Philippians 4:13 says I can do all things through Christ who strengthens me.

O LORD, I thank Thee for supplying all my needs in every predicament. I thank Thee for supplying my needs in the morning, afternoon and night. I am a victor over my circumstances and not a victim. I am a winner for all my needs will be supplied unto me. I am blessed by God because He has supplied all my needs wherever I may be.

I will not live in sorrow anymore. I am going to possess my possession. My God shall supply all my needs according to His riches in glory by Christ Jesus. No man or devil can stop God's blessing from coming to me because His word will not return void to Him. Rather it shall accomplish that which God has purposed and prosper.

I will be lifted up wherever I may be and wherever I may be, men and women will look for me and I will be blessed because the word of God says that the blessing of God adds no sorrow but makes one rich.

O LORD, bless me in season and out of season, in Jesus mighty name I pray. Amen.

Prayer For Breakthrough

But on Mount Zion there shall be deliverance, and there shall be holiness; the house of Jacob shall possess their possessions.

(Obadiah 1:17)

Now Jabez was more honourable than his brothers, and his mother called his name Jabez, saying, "Because I bore him in pain." And Jabez called on the God of Israel saying, "Oh, that You would bless me indeed, and enlarge my territory, that Your hand would be with me, and that You would keep me from evil, that I may not cause pain!" So God granted him what he requested.

(1 Chronicles 4:9-10)

The Hour Of Prayer

O LORD, I ask Thee to turn my weaknesses into strength. I ask Thee to turn my sorrow to joy. Turn my disgrace to grace. Turn my problems to promotion. Turn my frustrations to fulfilments. I ask Thee to renew my life. I ask Thee to make a way where there seems to be no way for me. I ask Thee to turn my captivity to victory.

According to Your word in Psalm 126:1-6 it says, "When the LORD brought back the captivity of Zion, we were like those who dream. Then our mouth was filled with laughter, and our tongue with singing. Then they said among the nations, "The LORD has done great things for them." The LORD has done great things for us, and we are glad. Bring back our captivity, O LORD, as the streams in the South. Those who sow in tears shall reap in joy. He who continually goes forth weeping, bearing seed for sowing, shall doubtless come again with rejoicing, bringing his sheaves with him."

I am going to breakthrough in every area of my life, in Jesus mighty name. Amen.

Beloved God's word says that all things work together for good to those who love Him.

The Hour Of Prayer

O LORD, I claim every prayer in this chapter, in Jesus mighty name. O LORD, I claim back whatever the enemies have stolen from me. I claim back my wealth from my enemies. I claim my position in ministry, business, and marriage, in Jesus Name.

Now, pray for seven things you want God to do for you. Pray for five minutes. Pray for others also.

PART 2

Different Kinds Of Prayers

Prayer Against The Devourer

Beloved, be sober and vigilant because the devil is roaming around, looking to whom he may devour. Let it be known to you that not everybody you see in this world is a human being. We need to cover ourselves with the blood of Jesus, through prayer so that we can overcome the works of the devil.

Do not love the world or the things of the world. The bible tells us that if anyone loves the world, the love of the Father is not in him. For all that is in the world - the lust of the flesh, the lust of the eyes, and the pride of life - is not of the Father but is of the world. And the world is passing away, and the lust of it, but he who does the will of God abides forever. Little children, it is the last hour; and as you have heard that the Antichrist is coming, even now many antichrists have come, by which we know that it is the last hour.

Prayer To Overcome The Habit Of Making Rash Promises To God

The word OVERCOME :

OBEDIENT	I want to be obedient to your word.
VICTORY	I want to be Victor over my enemies and not Victim of it.
ESTABLISH	I want to establish a good relationship with God.
RIGHTEOUSNESS	I want to live a righteous life in Jesus name.

COMMUNION	I will partake the Holy Communion in season and out of season.
OBTAIN FAVOUR	I will obtain favour from God
MIRACLE	My God is a working miracle God.
ENEMY	I will defeat all my enemies . In Jesus name. Amen.

These steps will help you to overcome every of your problem in Jesus Mighty Name.

Ecclesiastes 5:1-7 says, "Walk prudently when you go to the house of God; and draw near to hear rather than to give the sacrifice of fools, for they do not know that they do evil. Do not be rash with your mouth, and let not your heart utter anything hastily before God. For God is in heaven, and you on earth; therefore let your words be few. For a dream comes through much activity, and a fool's voice is known by his many words. When you make a vow to God, do not delay to pay it; for He has no pleasure in fools. Pay what you have vowed— Better not to vow than to vow and not pay. Do not let your mouth cause your flesh to sin, nor say before the messenger of God that it was an error. Why should God be angry at your excuse and destroy the work of your hands? For in the multitude of dreams and many words there is also vanity. But fear God."

O LORD, I ask Thee to give me the grace to fulfil all my vows in Jesus name. I ask Thee to forgive me for not fulfilling all my vows to you in the past. Thank You for answering my prayer. In Jesus name. Amen. Beloved, fulfil all the vows that you have made to God so that it will not hinder your prayers.

Prayer For Paying Your Tithes

The word TITHE :

TESTIFY   I will testify the benefit of paying tithes

INVOLVE	I will be involved in paying my tithes
TRUTHFULNESS	I will be truthful in paying my tithes
HONOUR	I will honour His word by paying my tithes.
ENEMY	The enemies cannot stop me from paying my tithes.

In Jesus mighty name. Amen.

Malachi 3:8-12 says, "Will a man rob God? Yet you have robbed Me! But you say, 'In what way have we robbed You?' In tithes and offerings. You are cursed with a curse, for you have robbed Me, even this whole nation. Bring all the tithes into the storehouse, that there may be food in My house, and try Me now in this," Says the LORD of hosts, "If I will not open for you the windows of heaven and pour out for you such blessing that there will not be room enough to receive it. And I will rebuke the devourer for your sakes, so that he will not destroy the fruit of your ground, nor shall the vine fail to bear fruit for you in the field," Says the LORD of hosts; And all nations will call you blessed, for you will be a delightful land," Says the LORD of hosts."

If you are not paying your tithe, you are robbing God. So, pay your tithes, in Jesus name.

O LORD, as from today, I will pay my tithes, wherever I may be. I will not hesitate to do so because it is settled in heaven that I should pay it so that the windows of heaven will be open for me. Lord, I want to be a blessing in paying my tithes. I thank Thee for answering my prayer in Jesus mighty name. Amen.

Beloved, you should pay your tithes. Your tithe is one-tenth of your income. For example, if you make a profit of 1,000 dollars, then one hundred dollars is your tithe to God.

Prayer For Helping The Poor

The word "POOR":

PEOPLE	I will be part of helping the poor people
OBSERVE	I will observe what the need and render help for them.
OBEY	I will obey His word by helping the needy
RESTORE	I will restore people's lives wherever they may be.
	In Jesus Mighty Name.

Isaiah 58:6-10 says, "Is this not the fast that I have chosen: To loose the bonds of wickedness, to undo the heavy burdens, to let the oppressed go free, and that you break every yoke? Is it not to share your bread with the hungry, and that you bring to your house the poor who are cast out; when you see the naked, that you cover him, and not hide yourself

from your own flesh? Then your light shall break forth like the morning, your healing shall spring forth speedily, and your righteousness shall go before you; the glory of the LORD shall be your rear guard. Then you shall call, and the LORD will answer; you shall cry, and He will say, 'Here I am.' If you take away the yoke from your midst, the pointing of the finger, and speaking wickedness, if you extend your soul to the hungry and satisfy the afflicted soul, then your light shall dawn in the darkness, and your darkness shall be as the noonday."

O LORD, Your word in Acts 10:38-39 tells us, "how God anointed Jesus of Nazareth with the Holy Spirit and with power, who went about doing good and healing all who were oppressed by the devil, for God was with Him. And we are witnesses of all things which He did both in the land of the Jews and in Jerusalem, whom they killed by hanging on a tree."

O LORD, as from today, I will render help to the poor. I will not wait for them to come to me for help before I would extend a helping hand.

I ask Thee to give me the grace to render help to them even before they come to me asking for help because your word says in Isaiah 58:7, *"Is it not to share your bread with the hungry, And that you bring to your house the poor who are cast out; When you see the naked, that you cover him."*

Apostle John said whoever hates his brother is a murderer, and you know that no murderer has eternal life abiding in him. By this, we know love because He laid down His life for us. And we also ought to lay down our lives for the brethren. But whoever has this world's goods, and sees his brother in need, and shuts up his heart from him, how does the love of God abide in him? My little children, let us not love in word or in tongue, but in deed and in truth. And by this, we know that we are of the truth, and shall assure our hearts before Him."

O LORD, as from today, I will exercise love towards the poor around me, in Jesus name. Amen.

Prayer For Your Marriage Life

The word LIFE:

LOVE	I will love my wife with all my heart.
INCREASE	I will increase the love I have for my wife.
FOLLOW	I will not follow another woman except my wife.
ESTABLISH	I will establish a good relationship with my wife.

He who finds a wife finds a good thing, and obtains favour from the LORD.

(Proverbs 18:22)

Wives, submit to your own husbands, as to the Lord. For the husband is head of the wife, as also Christ is head of the church; and He is the Saviour of the body.

(Ephesians 5:22-23)

This is a prayer for those who are looking for their partner in marriage

O LORD, thank You for my marriage life. O LORD, Your word says in Genesis 2:18, "And the LORD God said, "It is not good that man should be alone; I will make him a helper comparable to him."

Give me the grace to find the right person, wherever she/he may be, that you have set for me, to be my wife/husband in marriage. I decree that she/he will not have peace of mind until she/he finds me, in Jesus name. Amen.

Prayer For Married Couples

O LORD, bless our marriage life. O LORD, give us the grace to love each other. O LORD, let peace reign in our marriage life. Give us the grace to overcome every obstacle in our marriage life.

Separate the spirit of misunderstanding from us. Let our love for each other continue to grow stronger each day. Your word says in Colossians 3:18-19, *"Wives, submit to your own husbands, as is fitting in the Lord. Husbands, love your wives and do not be bitter toward them."*

I declare that we will continue to love each other in Jesus might name. Amen.

Pray for 5 minutes for others you know that are not married yet. Also, pray for those who need help in their marriage life so that peace will reign over them.

Galatians 6:1-2 says, "Brethren, if a man is overtaken in any trespass, you who are spiritual restore such a one in a spirit of gentleness, considering yourself lest you also be tempted. Bear one another's burdens, and so fulfil the law of Christ."

Prayer For The Fruit Of The Womb

The word WOMB:

WAITING UPON GOD	I will wait patiently for God to see me through.
OBEY	I will obey His word wherever I may be.
MEEKNESS	I will continue to be a meek person in the Lord.
BELIEVE	I believe if God will do it for others He will do it for me.

1 Samuel 1:11-20 tells us about Hannah. "Then she made a vow and said, "O LORD of hosts, if You will indeed look on the affliction of Your maidservant and remember me, and not forget Your maidservant, but will give Your maidservant a male child, then I will give him to the LORD all the days of his life, and no razor shall come upon his head." And it happened,

as she continued praying before the LORD, that Eli watched her mouth. Now Hannah spoke in her heart; only her lips moved, but her voice was not heard. Therefore Eli thought she was drunk. So Eli said to her, "How long will you be drunk? Put your wine away from you!" But Hannah answered and said, "No, my lord, I am a woman of sorrowful spirit. I have drunk neither wine nor intoxicating drink, but have poured out my soul before the LORD. Do not consider your maidservant a wicked woman, for out of the abundance of my complaint and grief I have spoken until now." Then Eli answered and said, "Go in peace, and the God of Israel grant your petition which you have asked of Him." And she said, "Let your maidservant find favour in your sight." So the woman went her way and ate, and her face was no longer sad. Then they rose early in the morning and worshipped before the LORD, and returned and came to their house at Ramah. And Elkanah knew Hannah his wife, and the LORD remembered her. So it came to pass in the process of time that

Hannah conceived and bore a son, and called his name Samuel, saying, "Because I have asked for him from the LORD."

O LORD, I was not born in sorrow. I was born to be blessed. O LORD, bless me like other women and let Your name be glorified. O LORD, restore my womb so that I can testify to others Your goodness. LORD, I will dedicate my child into Your kingdom and I will make every effort to see that the child will serve You. LORD, I thank You for answering my prayer, in Jesus mighty name. Amen.

Now, pray for others who you know are married but have no children. Pray for 5 minutes.

Prayer For Thanksgiving

Philippians 4:6 says, "Be anxious for nothing, but in everything by prayer and supplication, with thanksgiving, let your requests be made known to God."

Psalm 95:2 "Let us come before His presence with thanksgiving; Let us shout joyfully to Him with psalms."

Make a joyful shout to the LORD, all you lands! Serve the LORD with gladness; come before His presence with singing. Know that the LORD, He is God; it is He who has made us, and not we ourselves; we are His people and the sheep of His pasture. Enter into His gates with thanksgiving, and into His courts with praise. Be thankful to Him, and bless His name. For the LORD is good; His mercy is everlasting, and His truth endures to all generations."

The Hour Of Prayer

Praise the LORD! Sing to the LORD a new song, and His praise in the assembly of saints. Let Israel rejoice in their Maker; let the children of Zion be joyful in their King. Let them praise His name with the dance; let them sing praises to Him with the timbrel and harp. For the LORD takes pleasure in His people; He will beautify the humble with salvation. Let the saints be joyful in glory; let them sing aloud on their beds.

Let the high praises of God be in their mouth, and a two-edged sword in their hand, to execute vengeance on the nations, and punishments on the peoples"

Praise the LORD! Praise God in His sanctuary; praise Him in His mighty firmament! Praise Him for His mighty acts; praise Him according to His excellent greatness! Praise Him with the sound of the trumpet; praise Him with the lute and harp! Praise Him with the timbrel and dance. Praise Him with stringed instruments and flutes! Praise Him with loud cymbals; praise Him with clashing cymbals! Let everything that has breath praise the LORD. Praise the LORD!"

In Jesus mighty name we pray. Amen.

Beloved, it is vitally important to give thanks to the LORD for what He has done for us. Nehemiah gave thanks to the LORD after the walls of Jerusalem that were broken down have been rebuilt. Hannah also gave thanks to the LORD when Samuel was born. When Jesus was born, His mother Mary gave thanks to the LORD. There are many others who gave thanks to the LORD. So, offer your thanksgiving to the LORD, in season and out of season in Jesus Mighty Name.

Prayer To Know Your Vision

Proverbs 29:18 says, "Where there is no revelation, the people cast off restraint; But happy is he who keeps the law."

The Hour Of Prayer

O LORD, I need your manifestation, to know your vision for me. O LORD, I know that the call of God in my life is the first avenue of service and my skill or profession is the other avenue of service. O LORD, reveal to me every irrevealable that I may know my vision. I will not be carried away with the things of the world.

O LORD, I do not want to love the things of the world because Your word says do not love the world or the things in the world. If anyone loves the world the love of the Father is not in him. For all that is the world is the lust of the flesh, the lust of the eyes and the pride of the world. And the world is passing away and the lust of it, but he who does the will of God abides forever. Little children it is the last hour and as you have heard that the Antichrist is coming even now many Antichrist have come by which we know that it is the last hour.

Thank You LORD, for revealing to me my vision, in Jesus mighty name. Amen.

Prayer To Know Your Ministry

There are diversities of gifts, but the same Spirit. There are differences of ministries, but the same Lord. And there are diversities of activities, but it is the same God who works all in all. But the manifestation of the Spirit is given to each one for the profit of all: for to one is given the word of wisdom through the Spirit, to another the word of knowledge through the same Spirit, to another faith by the same Spirit, to another gifts of healings by the same Spirit, 10 to another the working of miracles, to another prophecy, to another discerning of spirits, to another different kinds of tongues, to another the interpretation of tongues. But one and the same Spirit works all these things, distributing to each one individually as He wills.

(1 Corinthians 12:4-11)

There are two types of ministries.

- Universal Ministry
- Ecclesiastical Ministry

O LORD, Your word says in Philippians 4:13 that I can do all things through Christ who strengthens me. 1 Corinthians 12:4-6 tells us, "There are diversities of gifts, but the same Spirit. There are differences of ministries, but the same Lord. And there are diversities of activities, but it is the same God who works all in all."

O LORD, I want to be part of it. O LORD, I do not want to occupy a position that does not belong to me. LORD show me what you have called me to be because many are called, few are chosen. O LORD, thank You for showing me the ministry that You have called me to hold, in Jesus name. Amen.

Prayer To Turn Your Weaknesses To Strength

Today, many continue to live in sin even though they attend church service every Sunday. But the bible tells us in Ezekiel 18:4, *"Behold, all souls are Mine; the soul of the father as well as the soul of the son is Mine; the soul who sins shall die."*

Your word says in Ezekiel 18:20, "The soul who sins shall die. The son shall not bear the guilt of the father, nor the father bear the guilt of the son. The righteousness of the righteous shall be upon himself, and the wickedness of the wicked shall be upon himself."

Ezekiel 33:8-9 tells us, "When I say to the wicked, 'O wicked man, you shall surely die!' and you do not speak to warn the wicked from his way, that wicked man shall die in his iniquity; but his blood I will require at your hand. Nevertheless if you warn the wicked to turn from his way, and he does not turn from his way, he shall die in his iniquity; but you have delivered your soul."

The Hour Of Prayer

O LORD, Your word says in 1 Corinthians 1:25-31, "For you see your calling, brethren, that not many wise according to the flesh, not many mighty, not many noble, are called. But God has chosen the foolish things of the world to put to shame the wise, and God has chosen the weak things of the world to put to shame the things which are mighty; and the base things of the world and the things which are despised God has chosen, and the things which are not, to bring to nothing the things that are, that no flesh should glory in His presence. But of Him you are in Christ Jesus, who became for us wisdom from God — and righteousness and sanctification and redemption that, as it is written, *"He who glories, let him glory in the LORD.""*

O LORD, I ask Thee to turn my weaknesses into strength. LORD, turn my sorrow to joy. O LORD, turn every temptation in my life to testimony.

O LORD, turn my bad to good. O LORD, turn my disgrace to grace. O LORD, turn my problems to promotions. I ask all these in Jesus name. Amen.

Prayer To Read And To Understand The Word Of God

O LORD, Your word says in Romans 10:17, "*So then faith comes by hearing, and hearing by the word of God.*"

Hebrews 4:12 says, "For the word of God *is* living and powerful, and sharper than any two-edged sword, piercing even to the division of soul and spirit, and of joints and marrow, and is a discerner of the thoughts and intents of the heart."

Your word says Mark 13:30-31, "*Assuredly, I say to you, this generation will by no means pass away till all these things take place.*" Heaven and earth *shall pass away but my words will by no means pass away."* O LORD, I ask Thee to give me the amazing ability to understand Your word. O LORD make a way in my life where there seems to be no way so that I will be impacted by Your word, wherever I may be.

O LORD, Your word says in Ephesians 6:10-17, "Finally, my brethren, be strong in the Lord and in the power of His might. Put on the whole armour of God, that you may be able to stand against the wiles of the devil. For we do not wrestle against flesh and blood, but against principalities, against powers, against the rulers of the darkness of this age, against spiritual hosts of wickedness in the heavenly places. Therefore take up the whole armour of God, that you may be able to withstand in the evil day, and having done all, to stand. Stand therefore, having girded your waist with truth, having put on the breastplate of righteousness, and having shod your feet with the preparation of the gospel of peace; above all, taking the shield of faith with which you will be able to quench all the fiery darts of the wicked one. And take the helmet of salvation, and the sword of the Spirit, which is the word of God."

O LORD, thank You for giving me the power to understand Your word. In Jesus mighty name. Amen.

Prayer To Speak In Tongues

And God has appointed these in the church: first apostles, second prophets, third teachers, after that miracles, then gifts of healings, helps, administrations, varieties of tongues. Are all apostles? Are all prophets? Are all teachers? Are all workers of miracles? Do all have gifts of healings? Do all speak with tongues? Do all interpret? But earnestly desire the best gifts. And yet I show you a more excellent way.

(1 Corinthians 12:28-31)

Beloved, nobody will make you speak in tongues unless you practice it.

O LORD, Your word says that it is not by might nor by power but by the power of the Holy Spirit to be able to speak in tongues, which is the heavenly language.

O LORD, do not let me be discouraged by anyone from speaking in tongues. For it is vitally important for us to speak in tongues so that the enemies of our lives will flee away.

LORD, send forth Your power, vitality and dynamism that will enable us to overcome every plan of the enemy that is distracting us from speaking in tongues. O LORD, thank You for transforming me to be a better person and giving me the grace to speak in tongues, in Jesus name. Amen.

Prayer To Love One Another

Apostle John said that whoever has this world's goods, and sees his brother in need, and shuts up his heart from him, how does the love of God abide in him? Let us not love in word or in tongue, but in deed and in truth. By this, we know that we are of the truth, and shall assure our hearts before Him.

And now abide faith, hope, love, these three; but the greatest of these is love.

(1 Corinthians 13:13)

O LORD, I ask Thee to give me the spirit of loving others because many are not showing true love. Many say that they love you today but tomorrow they will no show love you.

Many say they love you only when they are inside the church but when it is outside the church it is not so. O LORD, I ask Thee to give us the power to exercise love towards our brothers and sisters in

Christ, both in season and out of season. Let Your name be glorified.

O LORD, do not let the devil have control over us which will not prevent us from showing love towards our brothers and sisters in Christ, in Jesus name. Amen.

Prayer Against Discrimination

Beloved, today many do discriminate in church and also outside the church. Many only talk to people of their own race even though they are Christians. How can this be?

The bible says in Romans 2:11 that there is no partiality with God.

The Hour Of Prayer

O LORD, I ask Thee to give me the grace to welcome everyone I met. Let me not be carried away by the spirit of discrimination. O LORD, I ask

Thee to rebuke the spirit of discrimination in our midst. I want to welcome everyone with the love of Christ, regardless of who they are or where they come from.

LORD, let me behave as a good Christian should towards everyone around me because Your word says "For God so loved the world that He gave His only begotten Son, that whoever believes in Him should not perish but have everlasting life. For God did not send His Son into the world to condemn the world, but that the world through Him might be saved. "He who believes in Him is not condemned; but he who does not believe is condemned already, because he has not believed in the name of the only Begotten Son of God. And this is the condemnation, that the light has come into the world, and men loved darkness rather than light, because their deeds were evil."

In Jesus mighty name I pray. Amen.

Prayer To See The Face Of God

The word GOD:

GRACE	O Lord I need your divine grace to see your glory
OBEY	I ask Thee to give me the power to obey your word so I will see your glory
DELIVER	O Lord I need your divine grace to see your glory.

I ask Thee to give me the power to obey your word so I will see your glory. I want to be delivered from every plan of the enemies so that I will see your glory. In Jesus Mighty Name.

Matthew 5:8 says, "*Blessed are the pure in heart, for they shall see God.*" Genesis 17:1-2 says. "When Abram was ninety-nine years old, the LORD appeared to Abram and said to him, "I am Almighty God; walk before Me and be blameless. And I will make My covenant between Me and you, and will multiply you exceedingly."

O LORD, I believe in You and everything about You. I believe that you can reveal every irrevealable to me. O LORD, I want to see Your face which will cause me to know that You love me because I know that when a man's ways please the LORD, He will make even his enemies to be at peace with him.

O LORD, Your word says that all things work together for good to those who love You, to those who are called according to Your purpose. LORD, make a way in my life where there seems to be no way so that I will have victory over the enemy so that I will see Your face, in Jesus mighty name I pray. Amen.

Prayer To Perform Miracles

Apostle Paul said that God has appointed these in the church: first apostles, second prophets, third teachers, after that, miracles, then gifts of healings, helps, administrations, varieties of tongues.

Acts 19:11-12 say, "Now God worked unusual miracles by the hands of Paul, so that even handkerchiefs or aprons were brought from his body to the sick, and the diseases left them and the evil spirits went out of them."

O LORD, use me to perform tremendous miracles and let Your name be glorified. Use me in season and out of season so that when miracles are performed, many who do not know You will come to know You. Now use a handkerchief or an apron and pray for the sick wherever they may be. Pray also for yourself. In Jesus Mighty Name.

O LORD, use me to heal the sick and raise the dead. Use me to heal the broken-hearted. Use me to heal the blind, the deaf and the dumb because Your word says in Matthew 10:1 & 8, "And when He had called His twelve disciples to Him, He gave them power over unclean spirits, to cast them out, and to heal all kinds of sickness and all kinds of disease....Heal the sick, cleanse the lepers, raise the dead, cast out demons. Freely you have received, freely give."

Use me O LORD, to do greater works because Jesus said in John 14:12-14, says "Most assuredly, I say to you, he who believes in Me, the works that I do he will do also; and greater works than these he will do, because I go to My Father. And whatever you ask in My name, that I will do, that the Father may be glorified in the Son. If you ask anything in My name, I will do it."

I ask all these through Jesus Christ our Lord and Saviour. Amen.

Prayer To Increase Your Faith In God

The word FAITH:

FEAR NOT	I will not be afraid of my enemies
ABIDE	I will Abide by His word.
INCREASE	I will increase my faith in God.

TESTIFY   I will testify His goodness
HONOUR   I will honour His word.

The book of Hebrews said that faith is the substance of things hoped for, the evidence of things not seen. But without faith, it is impossible to please Him, for he who comes to God must believe that He is, and that He is a rewarder of those who diligently seek Him.

Ephesians 2:8 says, *"For by grace you have been saved through faith, and that not of yourselves; it is the gift of God."*

Hebrews 2:4 says, *"God also bearing witness both with signs and wonders, with various miracles, and gifts of the Holy Spirit, according to His own will."*

The Hour Of Prayer

O LORD, I need Your presence with me, wherever I may go so that my faith in You will continue to grow and increase each day. O LORD, manifest Your presence in me because it is not by might nor by power to increase my faith but by the power of the Holy Spirit.

O LORD, Apostle Paul told us in 1 Corinthians 3:6-7, "I planted, Apollos watered, but God gave the increase. So then neither he who plants is anything, nor he who waters, but God who gives the increase."

O LORD, I thank Thee for increasing me greatly in Jesus mighty name I pray. Amen.

For we walk by faith, not by sight.
(2 Corinthians 5:7)

Prayer For Grace

The word GRACE:

GOSPEL	I ask thee to give me the grace to preach the gospel.
REPENT	I ask thee to give me the grace

	to repent fully in you O Lord
ANOINTING	I want you O Lord to anoint me.
COMPLETE	I will be complete in God because the grace of God is sufficient in me.
ENJOY	I want to enjoy my Christian life.

O LORD, thank You for giving me the grace to do what You have called me to do in Jesus Mighty Name. O LORD, Your word says in 1 Corinthians 15:10, "But by the grace of God I am what I am, and His grace toward me was not in vain; but I laboured more abundantly than they all, yet not I, but the grace of God which was with me."

I want to labour more abundantly for You than others. O LORD, grace is unmerited favour which You have bestowed upon us. Let it be my portion, in Jesus name. Your word says in Ephesians 2:8, "For by grace you have been saved through faith, and that not of yourselves; it is the gift of God." Apostle

Paul said in 2 Corinthians 12:9, "And He said to me, "My grace is sufficient for you, for My strength is made perfect in weakness." Therefore most gladly I will rather boast in my infirmities, that the power of Christ may rest upon me."

> *But He gives more grace. Therefore He says: God resists the proud, but gives grace to the humble.*
>
> *(James 4:6)*

O LORD, the word GRACE stands for:

GREAT	I want to be great
RIGHTEOUS	I want to live a righteous life
ABIDE	I want to abide by Your word
CONFIDENCE	I want to have confidence in God
EXPOSED	I want to be exposed by God

I claim all these by His grace in Jesus name. Amen.

PART 3

Different Kinds Of Prayers

Prayer For Churches

And I also say to you that you are Peter, and on this rock I will build My church, and the gates of Hades shall not prevail against it. And I will give you the keys of the kingdom of heaven, and whatever you bind on earth will be bound in heaven, and whatever you loose on earth will be loosed in heaven."

(Matthew 16:18-19)

I now rejoice in my sufferings for you, and fill up in my flesh what is lacking in the afflictions of

Christ, for the sake of His body, which is the church, of which I became a minister according to the stewardship from God which was given to me for you, to fulfill the word of God.

(Colossians 1:24-25)

The Hour Of Prayer

O LORD, we give You all the glory and adoration for giving us the privilege to worship You in season and out of season, in the churches of this end time.

O LORD, Your word said that if two of you agree on earth concerning anything that they ask, it will be done for them by My Father in heaven. For where two or three are gathered together in My name, I am there in the midst of them." We ask Thee to give us the grace to be united because Apostle Paul said for as the body is one and has many members, but all the members of that one body, being many, are one body, so also is Christ. For by one Spirit we were all baptised into one body—whether Jews or Greeks, whether slaves or free—and have all been made to drink into one Spirit. For in fact the body is not one member but many."

We thank Thee for giving us the amazing ability to be one in Christ. Jesus said I am no longer in the world, but these are in the world, and I come to You. Holy Father, keep through Your name those whom You have given Me, that they may be one as We are."

Also, Jesus said, "that they all may be one, as You, Father, are in Me, and I in You; that they also may be one in Us, that the world may believe that You sent Me. And the glory which You gave Me I have given them, that they may be one just as We are one: I in them, and You in Me; that they may be made perfect in one, and that the world may know that You have sent Me, and have loved them as You have loved Me. "Father, I desire that they also whom You gave Me may be with Me where I am, that they may behold My glory which You have given Me; for You loved Me before the foundation of the world. O righteous Father! The world has not known You, but I have known You, and these have known that You sent Me. And I have declared to them Your name, and will declare it, that the love with which You loved Me may be in them, and I in them."

O LORD, today many churches are not in unity because of one thing or the other. You are the living God who is able to put things in order.

O LORD, we need peace in all the churches that believe in Jesus Christ. We pray that all the churches will be in unity in the body of Christ. In Jesus name. Amen.

Prayer For Nations

Then say to them, 'Thus says the Lord GOD: "Surely I will take the children of Israel from among the nations, wherever they have gone, and will gather them from every side and bring them into their own land; and I will make them one nation in the land, on the mountains of

Israel; and one king shall be king over them all; they shall no longer be two nations, nor shall they ever be divided into two kingdoms again."

(Ezekiel 37:21-22)

The Hour Of Prayer

O LORD, Your word said that for nation will rise against nation, and kingdom against kingdom. And there will be famines, pestilences, and earthquakes in various places. All these are the beginning of sorrows. "Then they will deliver you up to tribulation and kill you, and you will be hated by all nations for My name's sake. And then many will be offended, will betray one another, and will hate one another. Then many false prophets will rise up and deceive many. And because lawlessness will abound, the love of many will grow cold. But he who endures to the end shall be saved." We have seen that the word of God did not say it in vain that he that endures to the end shall be saved.

LORD, we ask Thee to give us the grace to endure for what is going on in this world. Today, there are many terrorist attacks all over the world. Many people have been initiated with the spirit of terrorism.

LORD send forth Your power, vitality and dynamism and let Your name be glorified in all nations of the earth. In Jesus name we pray. Amen.

Now, pray for 5 minutes for peace to reign in every nation of the earth, in Jesus name.

Prayer For Giving To God

Give, and it will be given to you: good measure, pressed down, shaken together, and running over will be put into your bosom. For with the same measure that you use, it will be measured back to you.

(Luke 6:38)

O LORD, give us the grace to give unto You. O LORD, Your word says in *2 Corinthians 9:6-10,* "But this *I say:* He who sows sparingly will also reap sparingly, and he who sows bountifully will also reap bountifully. *So let* each one *give* as he purposes in his heart, not grudgingly or of necessity; for God loves a cheerful giver. And God *is* able to make all grace abound toward you, that you, always having all sufficiency in all *things,* may have an abundance for every good work. As it is written: *"He has dispersed abroad, He has given to the poor; His righteousness endures forever."* Now may He who supplies seed to the sower, and bread for food, supply and multiply the seed you have sown and increase the fruits of your righteousness."

O LORD, many strong Christians do not like to give to the church. Many are holy on the outside but not on the inside. Many give only when they like to give. Many give because they are expecting something in return. Many are in a position to give big amounts to God but they are not willing to do so.

O LORD, turn their weaknesses into strength so that they will be moved to give something tangible to God, in Jesus name. Amen.

Beloved, give something of more value to God when you are in a position to do so.

And my God shall supply all your need according to His riches in glory by Christ Jesus.
(Philippians 4:19)

Prayer For Travelling

The Hour Of Prayer

O LORD, Your word says in Psalm 125:1-2, "Those who trust in the LORD are like Mount Zion, which cannot be moved, but abides forever. As the mountains surround Jerusalem, so the LORD surrounds His people From this time forth and forever."

LORD, send forth Your angel to guide me and protect me whenever I am travelling. O LORD, I need Your presence wherever I may be because the steps of a good and righteous man are ordered by the LORD and He delights in all his ways.

O LORD, give me the ability to overcome every plan of the enemy wherever I may be. Lead me and guide me so that I will know when is the right time to travel.

O LORD, make a way where there seems to be no way and let Your name be glorified in Jesus name. Amen.

Prayer To Pay All Your Debts

O LORD, Your word says that upon Mount Zion, there shall be deliverance. There shall be holiness and the people of Jacob shall possess their possessions.

O LORD, I ask Thee to supply my needs according to Your riches in glory by Christ Jesus. Enable me to pay all my debts in Jesus name.

O LORD, I am in too many debts, more than I can cope. O Lord I am owing my house rents, my business partner, loans and the monthly expenses that need to be paid.

O LORD, Your word says in 2 Kings 4:1-7, "A certain woman of the wives of the sons of the prophets cried out to Elisha, saying, "Your servant my husband is dead, and you know that your servant feared the LORD. And the creditor is coming to take my two sons to be his slaves." So Elisha said to her, "What shall I do for you? Tell me, what do you have in the house?" And she said, "Your maidservant has nothing in the house but a jar of oil." Then he said, "Go, borrow vessels from everywhere, from all your neighbours — empty vessels; do not gather just a few. And when you have come in, you shall shut the door behind you and your sons; then pour it into all those vessels, and set aside the full ones." So she went from him and shut the door behind her and her sons, who brought the vessels to her; and she poured it out. Now it came to pass, when the vessels were full, that she said to her son, "Bring me another vessel." And he said to her, "There is not another vessel." So the oil ceased. Then she came and told the man of God. And he said, "Go, sell the oil and pay your debt; and you and your sons live on the rest."

I ask Thee O LORD to multiply my financial blessing, and my business so that my debts can be paid, as you did to the widow mentioned in the above verses, in Jesus mighty name I pray. Amen.

Prayer For Making Use Of Your Gifts

For the wages of sin is death, but the gift of God is eternal life in Christ Jesus our Lord.

(Romans 6:23)

O LORD, Your word says in 2 Timothy 1:6-9, "Therefore I remind you to stir up the gift of God which is in you through the laying on of my hands. For God has not given us a spirit of fear, but of power and of love and of a sound mind. Therefore do not be ashamed of the testimony of our Lord, nor of me His prisoner, but share with me in the sufferings for the gospel according to the power of God, who has saved us and called us with a holy calling, not according to our works, but according to His own purpose and grace which was given to us in Christ Jesus before time began."

Give me the power to make full use of my gifts and let Your name be glorified. O LORD, use me to heal the sick and cleanse the lepers. Use me to restore the unsaved ones. Enable me to use Your gifts to perform tremendous miracles. Use me to raise the dead. O LORD, increase my greatness to the glory of Your name, with the gifts that You have bestowed on me.

In Jesus name I pray. Amen.

Do not neglect the gift that is in you, which was given to you by prophecy with the laying on of the hands of the eldership.

(1 Timothy 4:14)

For by grace you have been saved through faith, and that not of yourselves; it is the gift of God.

(Ephesians 2:8)

Prayer For Your Friends

Brethren, if a man is overtaken in any trespass, you who are spiritual restore such a one in a spirit of gentleness, considering yourself lest you also be tempted. Bear one another's burdens, and so fulfil the law of Christ.

(Galatians 6:1-2)

O LORD, a friend in need is a friend indeed. I want to pray for my friends who are not believers in Christ. Anyone who rejects God's grace to receive salvation through Christ would have made the biggest mistake in life.

O LORD, restore my friends, (speak their names) who are still living in the flesh. Your word says in Galatians 5:19-25, "Now the works of the flesh are evident, which are: adultery, fornication, uncleanness, lewdness, idolatry, sorcery, hatred, contentions, jealousies, outbursts of wrath, selfish ambitions, dissensions, heresies, envy, murders, drunkenness, revelries, and the like; of which I tell you beforehand, just as I also told you in time past, that those who practice such things will not inherit the kingdom of God. But the fruit of the Spirit is love, joy, peace, longsuffering, kindness, goodness, faithfulness, gentleness, self-control. Against such there is no law. And those who are Christ's have crucified the flesh with its passions and desires. If we live in the Spirit, let us also walk in the Spirit."

O LORD, do not let my friends be partakers of those who will not inherit the kingdom of God. O

LORD, restore all my friends so that their lives will be transformed in Jesus mighty name I pray. Amen

> *When the LORD brought back the captivity of Zion, we were like those who dream. Then our mouth was filled with laughter, and our tongue with singing. Then they said among the nations, "The LORD has done great things for them." The LORD has done great things for us, and we are glad. Bring back our captivity, O LORD, as the streams in the South.*
>
> *(Psalm 126:1-4)*

Prayer To Understand And To Know When God Speaks

O LORD, Your word says that greater is He, the Holy Spirit, who is in us than he who is in the world. LORD, I want to be a victor in understanding Your word.

O LORD, give me the amazing ability to know when You speak to me because the devil is a liar who comes to steal, kill and destroy.

O LORD, do not let me be deceived by any kind of voice that does not belong to You. O LORD, open my understanding and enable me to comprehend Your word wherever I may be.

O LORD, Your word says that those who put their trust in God shall be like Mount Zion that cannot be moved but abides forever.

O LORD, thank You for answering my prayers, in Jesus name. Amen.

Prayer For An Increase

O LORD, Your word says in 1 Corinthians 3:6-7, "I planted, Apollos watered, but God gave the increase. So then neither he who plants is anything, nor he who waters, but God who gives the increase."

O LORD, I ask Three to increase me greatly so that my destiny will be fulfilled. O LORD, give me the grace to be at the right place, at the right time because the steps of a good man are ordered by the LORD and He delights in all his ways.

O LORD, do not let the enemy put me to shame. Rather, let the enemies of my life be put to shame, in Jesus name. Let me increase greatly in season and out of season.

In Jesus mighty name I pray. Amen.

Prayer For Families

That the man of God may be complete, thoroughly equipped for every good work.

(2 Timothy 3:17)

The Hour Of Prayer

O LORD, Your word says in Genesis 12:3, "I will bless those who bless you, and I will curse him who curses you; and in you all the families of the earth shall be blessed."

LORD, restore the lives of all my family members wherever they may be. O LORD, let the fire of God destroy every spirit of my ancestors, bringing shame in my family, in Jesus name.

LORD, manifest Thy present in the midst of my family members so that Your name be glorified. LORD, let Your peace reign in my family so that they will come to be in unity. O LORD, transform the lives of all my family members wherever they may be, in Jesus name. Amen.

> *You are sons of the prophets, and of the covenant which God made with our fathers, saying to Abraham, 'And in your seed all the families of the earth shall be blessed.' To you first, God, having raised up His Servant Jesus, sent Him to bless you, in turning away every one of you from your iniquities."*
>
> *(Acts 3:25-26)*

Prayer To Have The Mind Of Christ

Let this mind be in you which was also in Christ Jesus, who, being in the form of God, did not consider it robbery to be equal with God, but made Himself of no reputation, taking the form of a bondservant, and coming in the likeness of men. And being found in appearance as a man, He humbled Himself and became obedient to the point of death, even the death of the cross.
(Philippians 2:5-8)

O LORD, I need the mind of Christ so that when people see me, they will see Jesus in me. O LORD, help me to imitate the characters of Jesus because He is my bridegroom and I am His bride and whoever desires such an intimacy with Him, He beckons.

O LORD, bless me in every area of my life. Bless me O LORD, both in season and out of season. Bless me so that Your name is glorified. Bless me in every predicament.

Bless me O LORD because the righteous shall flourish like a palm tree, in Jesus name. Amen.

Prayer For Favour

O LORD, I need Your divine favour because heaven and earth shall pass away but Your word remains the same. O LORD, Your word says that the righteous shall flourish like a palm tree. He shall grow like a cedar in Lebanon. He shall prosper in season and out of season.

Your word says in Proverbs 12:2, "A good man obtains favour from the LORD, but a man of wicked intentions He will condemn."

O LORD, give me the amazing ability to obtain favour wherever I may be. Let Your divine favour show up at the right place and at the right time. O LORD, manifest Your favour in every area of my life.

Thank You for answering my prayer, in Jesus mighty name. Amen.

Prayer For Understanding In Our Studies

O LORD, I ask Thee to open my understanding so that I will know how to study effectively. O LORD, give me the power and time to read my books and help me to know what I do not know.

O LORD, Your word says that faith comes by hearing and hearing by the word of God. O LORD, give me the amazing ability to cope with my studies in school and also to have the time to read Your word in Jesus mighty name I pray. Amen.

Examine yourselves as to whether you are in the faith. Test yourselves. Do you not know yourselves, that Jesus Christ is in you?—unless indeed you are disqualified. But I trust that you will know that we are not disqualified.

(2 Corinthians 13:5-6)

Prayer To Put Your Trust In God

O LORD, Your word said that those who trust in the LORD are like Mount Zion, which cannot be moved but abides forever. As the mountains surround Jerusalem, so the LORD surrounds His people from this time forth and forever. For the sceptre of wickedness shall not rest on the land allotted to the righteous, lest the righteous reach out their hands to iniquity. Do good, O LORD, to those who are good, and to those who are upright in their hearts. As for such as turn aside to their crooked ways, the LORD shall lead them away with the workers of iniquity. Peace be upon Israel!"

O LORD, do not let the devil put me to shame and do not let me go astray from Your word. O LORD, show forth Your power and vitality and let Your name be glorified wherever I may be.

O LORD, increase my faith in You so that I can continue to put my trust in You, in Jesus mighty name I pray. Amen.

Prayer To Be Complete In God

And also if anyone competes in athletics, he is not crowned unless he competes according to the rules.

(2 Timothy 2:5)

that the man of God may be complete, thoroughly equipped for every good work.

(2 Timothy 3:17)

Your word said in Philippians 1:6 that he who has begun a good work in you will complete it until the day of our Lord Jesus Christ.

LORD, make me a better person today. I want to be complete in You both in season and out of season. LORD, I want to be a person of integrity. Change my circumstances and bring me closer to You.

O LORD, You are my everything. I want to be complete in You in my ministry, in my faith and in fulfilling my vows, in winning souls for the kingdom of

God, in showing agape love, in Jesus mighty name I pray. Amen.

> *For in Him dwells all the fullness of the Godhead bodily; and you are complete in Him, who is the head of all principality and power.*
>
> *(Colossians 2:9-10)*

Prayer For Destiny

My destiny shall prosper in every predicament. My destiny shall prosper wherever I may be. My destiny shall locate my location. My destiny shall possess my possession. My destiny shall show up in season and out of season.

My destiny will come to pass wherever I may be. My destiny will make me a better person. My destiny will turn my sorrow to joy. My destiny will turn my disgrace to grace in Jesus name I pray. Amen.

PART 4

Different Kinds Of Prayers

Prayer To Break Every Chain Of Bondage

O LORD, the hour has come to break every chain of bondage in my business, marriage life, ministry health, children, grandchildren, families, friends, churches, pastors, ministers, in the name of Jesus.

O LORD, help me to overcome every spirit of hindrance in my life. Let them be broken in Jesus mighty name I pray. Amen.

Prayer For Breaking Every Yoke

I break every yoke in my business, marriage life, ministry, in Jesus name.

O LORD, Your word says in Obadiah 1:17, "But on Mount Zion there shall be deliverance, and there shall be holiness; the house of Jacob shall possess their possessions."

I shall possess my possession both in season and out of season. I shall locate my location wherever I may be. I shall not let the enemy take away my possession.

I shall defeat every plan of the enemy because the steps of a good and righteous man are ordered by God, and He delights in all his ways. I shall not die but live to declare the goodness of the LORD in my life, in Jesus name. Amen.

Prayer For Breaking Every Barrenness

O LORD, Your word says many are the afflictions of the righteous, but God will deliver him out of them all. Your word says in Psalm 34:17-18, "The righteous cry out, and the LORD hears and delivers them out of all their troubles. The LORD is near to those who have a broken heart, and saves such as have a contrite spirit."

O LORD, my righteousness is in Christ Jesus and because I am righteous, I shall flourish like a palm tree. I shall grow like a cedar in Lebanon. Those who are planted in the house of the LORD shall flourish in the courts of our God. They shall still bear fruits in old age. They shall be fresh and flourishing to declare that the LORD is upright in Jesus mighty name. Amen. Every barrenness in my family that is affecting my breakthrough, marriage life, ministry and business, I destroy in Jesus name. Amen.

Prayer For Churches To Be In Unity

The word CHURCH :

COVER	I cover every church by the blood of Jesus Christ
HELP	Every church must help each other
UNITY	Unity must take place in all the churches
RESIST	I resist every plan of the enemies in all churches
CONQUER	I conquer every plan of the enemies in all churches
HONOUR	Every church must honour God's word in Jesus Name.

For as the body is one and has many members, but all the members of that one body, being many, are one body, so also is Christ. For by one Spirit we were all baptized into one body— whether Jews or Greeks, whether slaves or free—and have all been made to drink into[a] one Spirit. For in fact the body is not one member but many.

(1 Corinthians 12:12-14)

The Hour To Pray

O LORD, Your word says that we are members of one body in Christ. But due to one thing or the other, many will turn against each other.

O LORD, Your word says in 1 Corinthians 12:28-31, "And God has appointed these in the church: first apostles, second prophets, third teachers, after that miracles, then gifts of healings, helps, administrations, varieties of tongues. Are all apostles? Are all prophets? Are all teachers? Are all workers of miracles? Do all have gifts of healings? Do all speak with tongues? Do all interpret? But earnestly desire the best gifts. And yet I show you a more excellent way."

Today, many do speak in tongue but there are also many who do not speak in tongues. Many believe in the five-fold ministry while others do not believe in it. Many like to criticise others who believe in the five-fold ministry.

O LORD, Your word says in Ephesians 4:11-12, "And He Himself gave some to be apostles, some prophets, some evangelists, and some pastors and teachers, for the equipping of the saints for the work of ministry, for the edifying of the body of Christ."

We give you our adoration and praise. Thank You for giving us the grace to be united as one in Jesus mighty name. Amen.

Prayer For Nations To Be In Unity

The word UNITY :

UNITED	Every nation will be united
NATION	No nations will rise against each other

INVOLVE	I will be involved by praying for all nations
THINK	No nation will think of fighting each other
YOKE	I break every yoke in every nation in Jesus Name

Unless the LORD builds the house, they labour in vain who build it; unless the LORD guards the city, the watchman stays awake in vain. It is vain for you to rise up early, to sit up late, to eat the bread of sorrows; for so He gives His beloved sleep.

(Psalm 127:1-2)

I cover every nation by the blood of Jesus Christ. Let every nation be in unity in season and out of season. O LORD, let peace reign in all the nations of the earth so that Your name be glorified in Jesus name. We come against every terrorist attack in Jesus name. Your word says When the Lord turn again the captivity of Zion we are them that dream dreams.

We ask Thee to restore our future and turn our captivity to victory so that all the nations will be united as one body in Christ Jesus. Amen.

Prayer For Restoration

The LORD is my shepherd; I shall not want. He makes me to lie down in green pastures; He leads me beside the still waters. He restores my soul; He leads me in the paths of righteousness for His name's sake. Yea, though I walk through the valley of the shadow of death, I will fear no evil; for You are with me; Your rod and Your staff, they comfort me. You prepare a table before me in the presence of my enemies; You anoint my head with oil; My cup runs over. Surely goodness and mercy shall follow me all the days of my life; and I will dwell[a] in the house of the LORD forever.

(Psalm 23:1-6)

The Hour Of Prayer

O LORD, restore my business, my ministry, my marriage life, my faith, my relationship with You and my commitment to You O LORD in Jesus Name.

LORD, I thank Thee for Your salvation in Jesus name. Your word says in Jeremiah 30:17-18, "'For I will restore health to you and heal you of your wounds,' says the LORD, 'Because they called you an outcast saying: "This is Zion; no one seeks her."' Thus says the LORD: 'Behold, I will bring back the captivity of Jacob's tents, and have mercy on his dwelling places; the city shall be built upon its own mound, and the palace shall remain according to its own plan."

O LORD, thank You for good health for indeed by Your stripes I am healed from every sickness and disease and when people see me, they will know that I believe in Christ Jesus. Amen.

Prayer To Set The Captives Free

The Hour Of Prayer

O LORD, Your word said when the LORD brought back the captivity of Zion, we were like those who dream. Then our mouth was filled with laughter, and our tongue with singing. Then they said among the nations, "The LORD has done great things for them." The LORD has done great things for us, and we are glad. Bring back our captivity, O LORD, as the streams in the South. Those who sow in tears shall reap in joy. He who continually goes forth weeping, bearing seed for sowing, shall doubtless come again with rejoicing, bringing his sheaves with him."

O LORD, I ask Thee to turn over my captivity to victory in business, marriage life, health, ministry, attitude, character, faith and hope in Jesus name. O LORD, let not my enemy put me to shame. Rather, let all my enemies be put to shame. For I believe that I am going to breakthrough, in Jesus name. My

LORD will supply all my needs according to His riches in glory by Christ Jesus. 2 Corinthians 10:3-6 says, "For though we walk in the flesh, we do not war according to the flesh. For the weapons of our warfare are not carnal but mighty in God for pulling down strongholds, casting down arguments and every high thing that exalts itself against the knowledge of God, bringing every thought into captivity to the obedience of Christ, and being ready to punish all disobedience when your obedience is fulfilled."

In Jesus mighty name I pray. Amen

Prayer Against Every Hindrance

Rest in the LORD, and wait patiently for Him; do not fret because of him who prospers in his way, because of the man who brings wicked schemes to pass. Cease from anger, and forsake wrath; do not fret—it only causes harm. For evildoers shall be cut off; but those who wait on the LORD, they shall inherit the earth.

(Psalm 37:7-9)

O LORD, You are great and greatly to be praised. LORD, Your word says that if God is for me who can be against me. No weapon formed against me shall prosper.

I come against every hindrance the enemies have set before me, against my business, my marriage, ministry and my commitment to God. O LORD, reveal all my enemies to me so that I will be able to differentiate them from my friends.

Your word says in Psalm 37:23-24, "The steps of a good man are ordered by the LORD, and He delights in his way. Though he fall, he shall not be utterly cast down; for the LORD upholds him with His hand."

PART 5

The Benefits Of Prayer

When we pray, it will quicken our mortal body. It is the living proof of God's miraculous wonders in us. It is vitally important for everybody to be a part of it. Prayer moves mountains.

According to the bible in Matthew 17:14-21 it says, "And when they had come to the multitude, a man came to Him, kneeling down to Him and saying, "Lord, have mercy on my son, for he is an epileptic and suffers severely; for he often falls into the fire and often into the water. So I brought him to Your disciples, but they could not cure him." Then Jesus answered and said, "O faithless and perverse generation, how long shall I be with you? How long shall I bear with you? Bring him here to Me." And Jesus rebuked the demon, and it came out of him; and the child was cured from that very hour. Then the disciples came to Jesus privately and said, "Why could we not cast it out?" So Jesus said to them, "Because of your unbelief; for assuredly, I say to you, if you have faith as a mustard seed, you will say to this mountain, 'Move from here to there,' and it will move; and nothing will be impossible for you. However, this kind does not go out except by prayer and fasting."

I will explain clearly the above verses. The disciples of Jesus could not cure the boy suffering from epileptic. Jesus admonished His disciples for their unbelief and told them to bring the boy to him. Then Jesus rebuked the demon from the boy and he was healed. The disciples of Jesus asked Him privately why they could not cast out the demon from the boy. See what Jesus said to His disciples in verse 20-21, "So Jesus said to them, "Because of your unbelief; for assuredly, I say to you, if you have faith as a mustard seed, you will say to this mountain, 'Move from here to there,' and it will move; and nothing will be impossible for you. However, this kind does not go out except by prayer and fasting.""

Beloved, obedient to His word will elevate us and bring us into His prominence. So the above verses are telling us that we should increase our prayer life wherever we may be. Do you know that in a week there are 168 hours and 10 percent of it is about 17 hours?

Beloved ask yourself this question and know how many hours you pray in a week. My life is full of testimonies. I used to get sick and had to be admitted to hospital very often. But when I discovered that by increasing my prayer life, I do not fall sick like I used to anymore. Today my life is a living testimony. For many years now I have not gone to the hospital or complain of any sickness. It is your faith in prayer that will enable you to receive your healing. If you can increase your prayer life no sickness will attack you, in Jesus name. I am not saying that you should not go to the doctors if you are sick but you need to exercise your faith in God.

EPILOGUE

We need to pray wherever we may be. We must pray because the devil comes to steal, kill and destroy. Do you know that not everyone you see on the road is a human being? The world is passing away and the lust of it; but he who does the will of God abides forever. It is the last hour and as you have heard that the Antichrist is coming, by which we know that it is the last hour. Many people are in a tormenting place. They will be saying, "Had I known, I would have done the right thing when I was still in the world."

The years of our life in this world is short and while we are still alive, we are given the opportunity to turn away from our sinful ways and follow the way of righteousness. My hope is that by reading this book, it will help you in your walk with God.

Beloved, be sober and vigilant because the devil is roaming around, looking to whom he may devour. Let it be known to you that not everybody you see in this world is a human being. We need to cover ourselves with the blood of Jesus, through prayer so that we can overcome the works of the devil.

Do not love the world or the things of the world. The bible tells us that if anyone loves the world, the love of the Father is not in him. For all that is in the world - the lust of the flesh, the lust of the eyes, and the pride of life - is not of the Father but is of the world. And the world is passing away, and the lust of it, but he who does the will of God abides forever. Little children, it is the last hour; and as you have heard that the Antichrist is coming, even now many antichrists have come, by which we know that it is the last hour.

WORD OF ENCOURAGEMENT

Prayer is not based on human mentality or human decision. Rather, it is inspired by God for us to pray. Remember, when Jesus went up to the mountain, He prayed. When Jesus went out to the wilderness, He prayed. Before Jesus went to the Cross, He prayed. The scriptures in Matthew 4:1-4 says, "Then Jesus was led up by the Spirit into the wilderness to be tempted by the devil. And when He had fasted forty days and forty nights, afterward He was hungry. Now when the tempter came to Him, he said, "If You are the Son of God, command that these stones become bread." But He answered and said, "It is written, 'Man shall not live by bread alone, but by every word that proceeds from the mouth of God.'"

Beloved, there is something I have come to know about prayer. After being prayerful, the devil would try to come to attack you one way or another but he will definitely fall because God is faithful beyond temptation. When it comes along our way, God will make a way of escape.

If the devil is not after you, that is to say, Christ is not in you. If our Lord Jesus was tempted by the devil after His forty days praying and fasting in the wilderness, then we who bear the mark of Jesus in us need not be surprised when the enemy also tries to attack us and he will fail in Jesus Mighty Name.

When the enemy is after you, let me tell you, it is when your spiritual muscle is strong and being developed. It is also when your faith in God is becoming stronger and stronger.

If the enemy is not after you how can you become great or what would you say or testify what God has done in your life? There are many people mentioned in the bible, who prayed before victory took place in their lives. Nehemiah prayed and that caused him to succeed in rebuilding the walls of Jerusalem that were broken down. Hannah prayed and that caused her to bear many children. Because of Elijah's prayer, all the false prophets in Israel were defeated and were killed. Jabez prayed and God turned things around in his life.

Apostle Peter wrote, "Who is he who will harm you if you become followers of what is good? But even if you should suffer for righteousness' sake, you are blessed. And do not be afraid of their threats, nor be troubled. But sanctify the Lord God in your hearts, and always be ready to give a defence to everyone who asks you a reason for the hope that is in you, with meekness and fear; having a good conscience, that when they defame you as evildoers, those who revile your good conduct in Christ may be ashamed. For it is better, if it is the will of God, to suffer for doing good than for doing evil. Beloved, do not think it strange concerning the fiery trial which is to try you, as though some strange thing happened to you; but rejoice to the extent that you partake of Christ's sufferings, that when His glory is revealed, you may also be glad with exceeding joy. If you are reproached for the name of Christ, blessed are you, for the Spirit of glory and of God rests upon you. On their part He is blasphemed, but on your part He is glorified. But let none of you suffer as a murderer, a thief, an evildoer, or as a busybody in other people's matters."

Do you know that God may not reveal His glory to you if the enemy is not after you? Do you know that the book of Acts tells us that Jesus appeared to Apostle Paul while he was in prison because of the enemy's threat? Still, that did not prevent him from doing what God has called him to do. Do you want God to appear to you? Then you should increase your prayer life wherever you may be.

I have a testimony to share with you. The joy of the Lord is my strength and every day I would pray in a strong voice. The neighbours were against me and tried to subdue me because of the way I prayed but to no avail. By then, by the special grace of God, every day I would be hearing the voice of God and also be seeing His glory. Why? It was because I prayed for many hours. Many like to talk big when they are in a restaurant but in the things of God they will not speak the possibilities in God.

Beloved, there is time for everything. Even on Sundays, many do not go for church service or listen to the sermons on television or radio. Let me tell you, no matter what the level of your condition is, there will be a solution to solve that problem. I hope you understand what I am saying. Do you know why I said this? I have seen the deaf and the dumb preached to the word of God, according to their understanding. I have seen many, even though they are disabled, still they endeavour to come to church service on time in their condition.

I know of a blind woman who used to live at my place. Do you know that even though she was very old but she would make every effort to be in church on time? On the last day, God will judge each person according to His own way. Before we die God already knew how He will judge each and every one us.

The word of God says, "casting all your care upon Him, for He cares for you" and "be sober, be vigilant; because your adversary the devil walks about like a roaring lion, seeking whom he may devour". Jesus said, "come to me all you who labour and are heavy laden and I will give you rest."

ABOUT THE AUTHOR

Evangelist Innocent Mokwe is one of the Nigerian Men of God whom God is using mightily to spread His word in the world today. He is an international preacher who has travelled to many countries to preach the word of God and God has used him to heal many people during his evangelism and also used him to expose the work of the devil in the world and in the kingdom of darkness. He is a prophet with a powerful anointing of the Holy Spirit. His anointed messages have brought hope to many men and women of all ages.

He is also a prolific writer and has written many books. He hopes that many will be inspired by the books that he has written which would help the reader to strengthen their faith in Christ and in their daily walk with God.

Evangelist Innocent Mokwe was brought up in a Christian family. At the age of 12, he saw a vision of heaven. Heaven was exactly what the bible described, a place of paradise. He saw angels and the streets were paved in gold and the buildings were also made of gold. Everything was shining with glitters. It was breathtaking.

It was during his college years that he began to mix with the wrong people and became influenced by his college friends. He started to smoke and drink and he would follow his college friends everywhere; even to pubs. He became weak in his faith and life became meaningless to him. After graduating from college, he went abroad to venture a new life. He continued to live an aimless life of smoking and drinking. Then in 1994, he was suddenly rushed to the hospital. All that cigarettes and alcohol and his reckless lifestyle have affected his health very badly. The doctors gave him several injections and caused him to sleep.

It was at the hospital while he was sleeping, he saw himself sitting on a chair and there were two angels holding him back from entering a tall iron gate. He saw another angel asking for his name and when he told the angel his name, the angel started to pray for him. He woke up after that and began to recover. God has saved him from death that day. His life began to change for the better and he became a new person. Life became meaningful to him and with God's help, he was able to drop all his bad habits. He no longer has any desire for the pleasures of this world. He began to have a personal relationship with God every day. The LORD told him to return to his country for a revival and so he went back to Nigeria and joined a ministry there and became an evangelist. Then he attended Pilgrim Bible College. He began to preach the gospel in his country. The LORD then told him to go and spread the gospel to other countries and led him to countries like Libya, Egypt, India, China, Cambodia, Thailand, Singapore, Malaysia and other countries.

For further enquiry you may send your email to:
evang632000@yahoo.com
imokwe63@yahoo.com.sg
mokeee1963@yahoo.com.sg

LIST OF OTHER BOOKS WRITTEN BY THE AUTHOR

- JONAH GO TO NINEVEH PART
- TORMENTING PLACE
- ACCOUNT OF WHAT HAPPENS IN THE KINGDOM OF DARKNESS PART 1
- ACCOUNT OF WHAT HAPPENS IN THE KINGDOM OF DARKNESS PART 2
- DO NOT LOVE THE THINGS OF THE WORLD
- IS YOUR LIFE A LIVING TESTIMONY
- IT SHALL COME TO PASS
- MIXED IN THE MULTITUDE
- TRUE GOSPEL
- SPIRIT APPARENT
- SOLDIERS OF CHRIST PART 1
- CRUCIFY YOUR FLESH
- ARE YOU READY TO FARM FOR JESUS
- DIVINE CONNECTION
- WE ARE HIS MASTER BUILDERS
- BE SENSITIVE TO HIS DIVINE DIRECTION

- SEVEN STEPS TO SUCCESS
- IT DOES NOT MATTER
- ARE YOU A JEPHTHAH OF THIS END TIME
- THE BENEFIT OF DEATH
- JONAH GO TO NINEVEH PART 2
- WHAT IS YOUR MINISTRY
- WHAT IS YOUR VISION
- WAITING UPON GOD
- ARISE AND SHINE
- DEEPER LIFE
- DOING GREATER WORKS FOR GOD
- WHAT IS YOUR PURPOSE
- SOLDIERS OF CHRIST PART 2
- DESTINY
- I AM GOING TO BREAKTHROUGH
- HYPOCRITICAL HOLINESS
- I SAW HEAVEN
- BE REDEEMED
- ABUNDANT GRACE
- HOW TO PURSUE YOUR GOAL

- ANOINTING
- SPIRITUAL MATURITY
- KINGDOM MENTALITY
- WE ARE ONE IN CHRIST
- WHO ARE WE TO JUDGE
- DETERMINING THE BEST SOLUTION TO YOUR PROBLEM
- PRAY UNTIL SOMETHING HAPPEN
- WHO IS YOUR HELPER
- COMPANION AND COMPASSION
- ATTITUDE
- HUMAN IDEAS
- MOTIVATION
- FEAR NOT
- MANAGEMENT ACTIVITIES
- SOCIAL INTERACTION
- EFFECTIVE GROUPS
- PRINCIPLES OF PARTICIPATION
- THE GOSPEL SHALL CONTINUE
- DIFFERENT KINDS OF PRAYERS

- CONFIRMATION
- THE FOOLISHNESS OF GOD IS WISER THEN MEN
- DON'T LABOUR IN VAIN
- MIRACLES
- UNDERSTANDING YOUR DREAMS
- THE GARMENT OF JESUS
- IS YOUR NAME WRITTEN IN THE BOOK OF LIFE
- THE APPOINTED TIME
- WORK OUT YOUR SALVATION
- THE STRATEGY OF DESTINY
- WORK OUT YOUR SALVATION
- THE STRATEGY OF DESTINY
- THE BENEFITS OF GIVING
- THE RAPTURE
- BE A PERSON OF INTEGRITY
- DISCOVER WHERE GOD HAS INSTORED YOUR BLESSINGS
- INCREASE YOUR FAITH IN GOD

- A LABOURER IS WORTHY OF HIS WAGES
- THERE IS HOPE
- ARE WE IN BONDAGE
- THE WORK OF THE HOLY SPIRIT
- A CITY SET ON A HILL CANNOT BE HIDDEN
- FULFIL YOUR MINISTRY
- THERE IS TIME FOR EVERYTHING
- THIS IS A FAITHFUL SAYING
- WHO IS ON THE LORD S SIDE
- WISDOM
- FOUNDATION IN CHRIST
- FEAR THE LORD
- DIFFERENT KINDS OF FAITH

www.ingramcontent.com/pod-product-compliance
Lightning Source LLC
Chambersburg PA
CBHW071354080526
44587CB00017B/3096